WIX MASTERY

Build Stunning Websites with Ease

Peter Herzog

Copyright © 2024 Peter Herzog

All rights reserved. No part of this publication may be reproduced, distributed, or transmitted in any form or by any means, including photocopying, recording, or other electronic or mechanical methods, without the prior written permission of the publisher, except in the case of brief quotations embodied in critical reviews and certain other noncommercial uses permitted by copyright law.

FOREWORD

In today's fast-paced digital world, having an online presence is no longer a luxury but a necessity. Whether you're a small business owner, a freelancer, or someone with a passion project, a professional website can make all the difference. Yet, for many, the thought of creating a website is daunting, filled with technical jargon and complex coding requirements. This is where Wix comes into play, revolutionizing the way we build websites by offering a user-friendly platform that caters to all skill levels.

When I first embarked on my journey into web development, I faced numerous challenges and steep learning curves. Back then, creating a website was an intricate process that required substantial technical expertise. The advent of website builders like Wix has democratized web design, making it accessible to anyone with a vision and a willingness to learn.

Wix Mastery: Build Stunning Websites with Ease is a book that embodies this spirit of accessibility and empowerment. {{Peter Herzog}}, a seasoned expert in the field, has crafted a guide that breaks down the complexities of web design into manageable, easy-to-follow steps. This book is not just for the tech-savvy but for anyone eager to create a compelling online presence.

Throughout these pages, you'll find a wealth of knowledge that reflects years of experience and a deep understanding of the Wix platform. From setting up your first site to incorporating advanced features, every chapter is designed to equip you with the skills you need to build a website that truly stands out.

As you delve into this book, you'll appreciate its practical approach and clear explanations. The step-by-step instructions, coupled with insightful tips, ensure that you can navigate the Wix platform with confidence. Whether you're looking to create a simple blog, an online store, or a sophisticated business site, Mastering Wix provides the tools and knowledge to bring your vision to life.

I am confident that this book will serve as an invaluable resource for both beginners and seasoned web designers. It is a testament to the power of technology to simplify and enhance our creative processes. I invite you to embark on this journey with {{Peter Herzog}} and discover the endless possibilities that Wix has to offer.

Happy building!

INTRODUCTION

As the world becomes increasingly interconnected, the ability to effectively communicate and showcase one's brand, products, or services through a well-designed website has become an indispensable asset.

However, the process of creating a professional and visually appealing website can be daunting, especially for those without technical expertise or coding knowledge. Traditional website development often requires a significant investment of time, resources, and expertise, making it inaccessible for many.

Recognizing this challenge, innovative website-building platforms have emerged, offering user-friendly solutions that empower individuals and businesses to create stunning websites without the need for extensive coding knowledge. One such platform that has garnered widespread acclaim is Wix, a powerful yet intuitive tool that simplifies the website creation process while delivering professional-grade results.

Wix Mastery: Build Stunning Websites with Ease is a comprehensive guide that takes readers on a journey through the world of Wix, unveiling its capabilities and equipping them with the knowledge and skills necessary to create a website that truly stands out. From the initial setup to advanced customization and optimization, this book leaves no stone unturned, ensuring that readers can harness the full potential of this remarkable platform.

Through clear and concise explanations accompanied by real-world examples and practical exercises, Wix Mastery: Build Stunning Websites with Ease demystifies the website creation process, making it accessible to individuals of all skill levels. Whether you're a complete beginner or have some experience with website building, this book will serve as an invaluable resource, guiding you step-by-step through the process of creating a visually stunning and highly functional website.

One of the key strengths of 'Wix Mastery: Build Stunning Websites with Ease' lies in its comprehensive coverage of Wix's extensive feature set. From designing visually appealing layouts and incorporating multimedia elements to optimizing for search engines and ensuring mobile responsiveness, this book equips readers with the knowledge and tools necessary to create a website that truly resonates with their target audience.

Moreover, 'Wix Mastery: Build Stunning Websites with Ease' addresses common shortcomings identified in the reviews, such as providing detailed instructions for advanced features like adding headers, footers, and optimizing for mobile devices, as well as in-depth coverage of creating an online store.

Whether you're an entrepreneur seeking to establish an online presence for your business, a creative professional showcasing your portfolio, or an individual aiming to share your passion with the world, 'Wix Mastery: Build Stunning Websites with Ease' is your ultimate guide to website creation success. Embrace the power of Wix and let this handbook be your companion on the journey to building a website that truly represents you or your business.

CHAPTER ONE: GETTING STARTED WITH WIX

Introduction to Wix

In the ever-evolving digital landscape, having a robust online presence has become an indispensable asset for businesses and individuals alike. However, the process of creating a professional and visually appealing website can be daunting, especially for those without technical expertise or coding knowledge. Recognizing this challenge, Wix emerges as a powerful and user-friendly website-building platform that empowers anyone to create stunning websites without the need for extensive coding skills.

Wix is a cloud-based platform that provides a comprehensive suite of tools and features to design, build, and manage websites with ease. From stunning templates to a drag-and-drop editor, Wix simplifies the website creation process, making it accessible to individuals of all skill levels. Whether you're a small business owner, entrepreneur, artist, or hobbyist, Wix offers a seamless solution to establish your online presence.

Benefits of using Wix

1. **No Coding Required**: With Wix, you can bid farewell to the complex world of coding. The platform's intuitive drag-and-drop interface empowers you to create visually appealing websites without the need for extensive technical knowledge or programming skills.

2. **Responsive Design**: In today's mobile-centric world, having a website that adapts seamlessly to different devices is essential. Wix's responsive design feature ensures that your website looks great and functions flawlessly across desktops, tablets, and smartphones, providing a consistent user experience for your visitors.

3. **Comprehensive Design Tools**: Wix offers a vast array of design tools and customization options, allowing you to unleash your creativity and craft a website that truly reflects your brand or personal style. From templates and layouts to fonts, colors, and multimedia elements, you have complete control over the look and feel of your website.

4. **E-Commerce Functionality**: If you're looking to sell products or services online, Wix's e-commerce capabilities make it easy to create an online store. You can manage your inventory, accept secure payments, and streamline the entire shopping experience for your customers.

5. **Search Engine Optimization (SEO)**: Optimizing your website for search engines is crucial for attracting organic traffic and improving online visibility. Wix provides built-in SEO tools and guidelines to help you optimize your website's

content, structure, and metadata for better search engine rankings.

6. **Analytics and Insights**: Understanding your website's performance and visitor behavior is key to making informed decisions. Wix offers powerful analytics tools that provide valuable insights into traffic sources, popular pages, and user interactions, empowering you to continually improve and optimize your online presence.

System Requirements

Wix is a cloud-based platform, which means you don't need to install any software on your local machine. All you need is a modern web browser and a stable internet connection. Wix is compatible with most popular browsers, including Google Chrome, Mozilla Firefox, Safari, and Microsoft Edge.

While Wix can run on various devices, including desktops, laptops, tablets, and smartphones, it's recommended to use a larger screen for an optimal website editing and design experience.

Creating an account

Getting started with Wix is incredibly straightforward. Simply visit the Wix website (www.wix.com) and click on the "Get Started" button. From there, you'll be prompted to create a new account by providing your email address and creating a password.

Once your account is created, you'll be guided through a series of steps to help you personalize your website's purpose, choose a template, and begin the design process. Wix also offers the option to connect your website to a custom domain name, further enhancing your online presence and professionalism.

Understanding the Interface

Wix's user interface is designed to be intuitive and user-friendly, making it easy for anyone to navigate and utilize its features effectively. Upon logging into your account, you'll be greeted by the Wix Editor, which serves as the central hub for building and managing your website.

The Wix Editor consists of several key components:

1. **Workspace**: This is the main canvas where you'll design and arrange the elements of your website. You can drag and drop various components, such as text boxes, images, and multimedia elements, to create your desired layout.

2. **Toolbar**: The toolbar provides quick access to commonly used tools and features, including undo/redo actions, previewing your website, and publishing changes.

3. **Sidebar**: The sidebar contains a wide range of elements, such as media, design elements, and apps, that you can easily add to your website by dragging and dropping them onto the workspace.

4. **Settings Panel**: The settings panel allows you to customize various aspects of your website, including site structure, navigation, background settings, and more.

Wix's interface is designed to be intuitive and user-friendly, with tooltips and guidance available throughout the editing process. As you explore and familiarize yourself with the interface, you'll gain confidence in navigating its features and unleashing your creative potential.

CHAPTER TWO: PLANNING AND DESIGNING YOUR WEBSITE

Defining Your Website Goals

A clear understanding of what you aim to achieve with your online presence will guide your decision-making process and ensure that your website effectively serves its intended purpose.

Some common goals for websites include:

1. **Establishing an Online Presence**: If your primary objective is to establish an online presence for your business, brand, or personal endeavor, your website should serve as a virtual storefront, showcasing your offerings and providing visitors with essential information.

2. **Generating Leads and Sales**: For businesses seeking to generate leads and drive sales, your website should be designed with a strong emphasis on conversion optimization. This may include features like lead capture forms, e-

commerce functionality, and clear calls-to-action.

3. **Sharing Information and Resources**: If your goal is to share valuable information, resources, or educational content with your audience, your website should prioritize a user-friendly navigation structure and content organization.

4. **Building an Online Community**: If you aim to foster an online community around a specific interest or topic, your website should facilitate engagement and interaction through features like forums, social media integration, and user-generated content.

5. **Showcasing a Portfolio**: For creatives, artists, or professionals seeking to showcase their work, your website should serve as a visually appealing and well-organized portfolio, highlighting your skills and accomplishments.

Clearly defining your website goals will influence various aspects of your design and development process, such as the overall layout, navigation structure, content strategy, and functionality. By keeping your goals at the forefront, you can ensure that your website effectively meets the needs and expectations of your target audience.

Conducting market research

Before diving into the design and development of your website, it's essential to conduct thorough market research. This process will provide valuable insights into your target audience, competitors, and industry trends, enabling you to create a website that resonates with your audience and stands out in a crowded online landscape.

Market research can include:

1. **Target Audience Analysis**: Understanding your target audience is crucial for creating a website that meets their needs and preferences. Gather demographic information, such as age, location, interests, and online behavior, to tailor your website's content, design, and functionality accordingly.

2. **Competitor Analysis**: Analyze the websites of your competitors to identify their strengths, weaknesses, and unique selling propositions. This will help you differentiate your website and capitalize on opportunities to outperform your competition.

3. **Industry Trends**: Stay up-to-date with the latest trends and best practices in web design, user experience, and digital marketing. This knowledge will ensure that your website remains relevant and aligns with industry standards.

4. **User Feedback and Testing**: Gather feedback from potential users or conduct usability testing to understand their preferences, pain points, and expectations. This invaluable input can guide the design and functionality of your website.

Effective market research will provide you with a solid foundation for creating a website that resonates with your target audience, addresses their needs, and stands out in a competitive market.

Creating a Sitemap

A well-structured sitemap is essential for organizing your website's content and ensuring a seamless user experience. A sitemap acts as a blueprint for your website, outlining the hierarchy and relationships between different pages and sections.

When creating a sitemap, consider the following best practices:

1. **Main Navigation**: Identify the primary sections or categories that will make up your main navigation menu. These should be the most important and broad topics or areas of your website.

2. **Subsections and Pages**: Under each main navigation category, list the subsections or specific pages that will be included. This will help you organize your content in a logical and intuitive manner.

3. **Hierarchy and Structure**: Establish a clear hierarchy within your sitemap, with main sections at the top level and subsections and pages nested beneath them. This structure should reflect the importance and relationship of the content.

4. **User Flow**: Consider the natural flow and progression of how users will navigate through your website. The sitemap should facilitate a smooth and intuitive journey from one page to the next.

5. **Future Growth**: Leave room for future expansion and growth within your sitemap. As your website evolves, you may need to add new sections or pages, so it's important to have a flexible structure in place.

By creating a comprehensive sitemap, you'll not only organize your content effectively but also ensure that search engines can easily crawl and index your website, improving its visibility and search engine rankings.

Choosing a Website Layout

The layout of your website plays a crucial role in establishing a visually appealing and user-friendly experience. The right layout can enhance navigation, convey your brand's personality, and create a cohesive and engaging atmosphere for your visitors.

When choosing a website layout, consider the following factors:

1. **Purpose and Goals**: Align your layout with the primary purpose and goals of your website. For example, a portfolio website may benefit from a visually-driven layout, while an e-commerce site may require a more structured and product-focused design.

2. **User Experience**: Prioritize layouts that provide an intuitive and seamless user experience. Ensure that the navigation is clear, the content is easily accessible, and the overall design is responsive across different devices.

3. **Branding and Visual Identity**: Your website's layout should reflect and reinforce your brand's visual identity. Incorporate your brand colors, typography, and design elements consistently throughout the layout to create a cohesive and memorable experience.

4. **Content Hierarchy**: Consider the hierarchy and organization of your content when selecting a

layout. The layout should guide users' attention to the most important information and facilitate easy scanning and navigation.

5. **Trends and Best Practices**: Stay informed about current web design trends and best practices. While it's important to maintain a unique and distinctive layout, adhering to established guidelines can enhance usability and accessibility.

Popular website layout styles include grid-based layouts, single-page designs, minimal layouts, and more. Ultimately, the layout you choose should strike a balance between aesthetics, functionality, and alignment with your website's goals and target audience.

Incorporating branding elements

Your website is often the first touchpoint for potential customers or clients, making it crucial to incorporate strong branding elements that effectively communicate your brand's identity and values. A well-branded website not only creates a cohesive and memorable experience but also helps to establish trust and credibility with your audience.

Here are some key elements to consider when incorporating branding into your website:

1. **Logo and Brand Colors**: Your logo and brand colors should be prominently displayed on your website, acting as a visual anchor and reinforcing your brand's identity. Ensure that the logo is easily recognizable and that the brand colors are used consistently throughout the design.

2. **Typography and Fonts**: Carefully select the fonts and typography styles that align with

your brand's personality and tone. Consistent use of these elements across your website will contribute to a cohesive and professional appearance.

3. **Imagery and Graphics**: Incorporate high-quality imagery and graphics that represent your brand's values and offerings. These visual elements should be consistent with your brand's overall aesthetic and help to create a memorable and engaging experience for visitors.

4. **Brand Messaging and Tone**: Ensure that the language and tone used throughout your website's content accurately reflect your brand's voice and messaging. This consistency will help to reinforce your brand's identity and resonate with your target audience.

5. **Brand Story and Values**: Share your brand's story, mission, and values prominently on your website. This not only humanizes your brand but also helps to build a connection with visitors and establish trust and credibility.

By effectively incorporating branding elements throughout your website, you'll create a cohesive and memorable online presence that accurately represents your brand's identity and values, ultimately enhancing your credibility and resonating with your target audience.

CHAPTER THREE: BUILDING THE FOUNDATION

Creating a new website

With Wix, creating a new website is a straightforward process that can be accomplished in just a few simple steps. Whether you're starting from scratch or have an existing website, Wix provides a user-friendly interface that guides you through the initial setup process.

To create a new website, follow these steps:

1. **Log in to Your Wix Account**: If you haven't already, sign up for a free Wix account by visiting the Wix website and providing your email address and a password.

2. **Choose Your Website Type**: Upon logging in, you'll be prompted to select the type of website you want to create. Wix offers a variety of options, including online stores, blogs, portfolios, and more. Choose the option that best fits your needs.

3. **Answer a Few Questions**: Wix will ask you a series of questions to better understand your goals and preferences for your new website.

These questions may include the purpose of your website, your industry, and your preferred design style.

4. **Select a Starting Point**: Based on your answers, Wix will provide you with several options to start building your website. You can choose to start with a blank canvas and build your website from scratch or select a pre-designed template that aligns with your goals and preferences.

5. **Customize Your Website**: Once you've selected your starting point, you'll be taken to the Wix Editor, where you can begin customizing your website. This powerful editor allows you to easily modify the layout, add content, and adjust design elements to create a unique and professional-looking website.

Throughout the process of creating a new website, Wix provides helpful prompts, tooltips, and guidance to ensure a smooth and intuitive experience. Additionally, Wix offers a vast library of resources, including tutorials, forums, and support channels, to assist you with any questions or challenges you may encounter.

Selecting a Template

One of the greatest advantages of using Wix is the extensive collection of stunning, pre-designed templates available to users. These templates serve as a solid foundation for your website, providing a professional and visually appealing starting point that can be easily customized to suit your specific needs.

When selecting a template, consider the following factors:

1. **Industry and Purpose**: Wix offers templates tailored to various industries and purposes, such as business, portfolio, online store, photography, and more. Choose a template that aligns with the primary goal and focus of your website.

2. **Design and Aesthetics**: Browse through the available templates and select one that resonates with your brand's visual identity and design preferences. Consider factors such as color schemes, layout, and overall aesthetic appeal.

3. **Responsiveness**: Ensure that the template you choose is mobile-responsive, meaning it will adapt seamlessly to different screen sizes and devices, providing an optimal user experience for visitors accessing your website from smartphones or tablets.

4. **Customization Potential**: While templates provide a solid starting point, you'll likely want to customize them to make your website truly unique. Look for templates that offer flexibility and customization options, allowing you to modify layouts, colors, fonts, and other design elements.

Once you've selected a template, Wix's intuitive editor allows you to easily customize and tailor it to your specific requirements, ensuring that your website stands out and accurately represents your brand or personal style.

Customizing the template

While Wix templates provide an excellent foundation for your website, the true power lies in your ability to customize and personalize them to create a unique and distinct online presence. Wix's user-friendly editor offers a wide range of customization options, allowing you to tweak every aspect of your website to align with your brand's identity and goals.

Here are some key areas you can focus on when customizing your Wix template:

1. **Layout and Structure**: Wix's drag-and-drop interface makes it easy to rearrange the layout of your website pages. You can add, remove, or reposition sections, columns, and elements to create a layout that best suits your content and user experience goals.

2. **Branding and Design**: Customize the visual elements of your website to reflect your brand's identity. This includes changing colors and fonts, adding your logo, and incorporating brand-specific graphics or images.

3. **Content and Multimedia**: Add and format text, images, videos, and other multimedia content to convey your message effectively. Wix offers a wide range of tools and options to help you create engaging and visually appealing content.

4. **Navigation and Menus**: Customize the navigation menus to ensure that visitors can easily find and access the most important pages and sections of your website. Wix allows you to create clear and intuitive navigation structures, including dropdowns and mega menus.

5. **Interactive Elements**: Enhance user engagement by incorporating interactive elements such as forms, surveys, slideshows, and animations.

These features can not only make your website more dynamic but also help you capture leads and gather valuable user data.

6. **Mobile Optimization**: Ensure that your website looks and functions flawlessly on mobile devices by utilizing Wix's mobile optimization tools. You can preview and adjust the mobile view, ensuring a seamless experience for visitors accessing your website from smartphones or tablets.

Throughout the customization process, Wix's editor provides helpful prompts, tooltips, and resources to guide you through various features and functionalities. Additionally, Wix's extensive library of apps and integrations allows you to further enhance your website's capabilities and tailor it to your specific needs.

Adding Pages

As you build your website, you'll likely need to create multiple pages to organize and showcase different types of content or information. Wix makes it easy to add new pages and manage your website's structure and navigation.

Here are the key steps to adding pages to Wix:

1. **Access the Page Manager**: Within the Wix Editor, locate the "Pages" or "Menus & Pages" section, typically found in the left-hand sidebar or settings panel. This is where you can manage and add new pages to your website.

2. **Create a New Page**: Click on the "Add Page" or "+" button to create a new page. You may be prompted to select a layout or template for your new page, or you can start with a blank canvas.

3. **Name and Organize**: Give your new page a descriptive and relevant name that accurately reflects its content or purpose. You can also organize your pages into different sections or categories by creating subpages or nested structures.

4. **Add Content**: Once your new page is created, you can start adding content to it using Wix's intuitive drag-and-drop editor. Add text, images, videos, forms, and other elements to build out your page's content and design.

5. **Set Page Settings**: Wix provides various settings and options for each page, allowing you to customize the page's behavior, appearance, and functionality. This includes setting the page's SEO properties, enabling or disabling comments, and adjusting the page's layout and styling.

6. **Link and Navigate**: After adding your new page, ensure that it's properly linked and accessible from your website's navigation menu. You can easily add or remove pages from your main menu or create custom navigation structures within Wix's editor.

Throughout the process of adding pages, Wix offers helpful tooltips, guidance, and resources to ensure a smooth and efficient workflow. Additionally, you can preview your website at any time to see how your new pages integrate with the overall design and structure of your site.

Navigating the Editor

Wix's intuitive and user-friendly editor is the heart of the website-building process, providing a comprehensive set of tools and features to create and customize your online presence. While the editor may seem daunting at first glance, its well-designed interface and helpful resources make it accessible to users of all skill levels.

Here are some key elements and features of the Wix Editor:

1. **Workspace**: The workspace is the main canvas where you can design and arrange the elements of your website. It provides a visual representation of how your website will look and allows you to drag and drop various components, such as text boxes, images, and multimedia elements.

2. **Sidebar**: The sidebar contains a wide range of elements and tools that you can easily add to your website by dragging and dropping them onto the workspace. This includes media elements, design components, apps, and more.

3. **Toolbar**: The toolbar provides quick access to commonly used tools and features, such as undo/redo actions, previewing your website, publishing changes, and accessing helpful resources.

4. **Settings Panel**: The settings panel allows you to customize various aspects of your website, including site structure, navigation, background settings, and more. It also provides access to advanced features and integrations.

5. **Tooltips and Guidance**: Throughout the editor, Wix provides helpful tooltips and guidance to assist you with various tasks and features. These tooltips offer explanations, tips, and step-by-step instructions, ensuring a smooth learning

experience.

6. **Previewing and Responsiveness**: Wix's editor allows you to preview your website in real-time, ensuring that you can see how your changes will appear on different devices and screen sizes. This feature is crucial for ensuring that your website is responsive and provides an optimal user experience across various platforms, including desktops, tablets, and smartphones. You can easily switch between desktop, tablet, and mobile views within the editor, making it simple to identify and address any potential layout or formatting issues. Additionally, Wix's mobile optimization tools allow you to make specific adjustments to the mobile version of your site, ensuring a seamless experience for users accessing your website on the go.

7. **Undo/Redo**: The undo and redo buttons in the toolbar provide a convenient way to quickly reverse or reapply any changes you make within the editor. This feature can be particularly helpful when experimenting with different design or layout options, allowing you to easily revert to a previous state if needed.

8. **Help and Resources**: Wix offers a wealth of resources and support materials to assist you throughout the website-building process. Within the editor, you can access video tutorials, written guides, and a comprehensive knowledge base to learn more about specific features or troubleshoot any issues you may encounter.

9. **Collaboration and Sharing**: If you're working on a website project with others, Wix's collaboration and sharing features allow you to invite team members or clients to view and provide feedback on your work in progress. This streamlined collaboration process can help ensure that everyone is on the same page and that your website meets the desired requirements.

10. **Publishing and Updates**: Once you've completed your website design and are satisfied with the results, Wix's publishing tools make it easy to launch your site and share it with the world. Additionally, Wix provides seamless update mechanisms, ensuring that your website remains up-to-date and benefits from the latest features and security enhancements.

By understanding and utilizing the various elements and features of the Wix Editor, you'll be able to navigate the website-building process with confidence and create a professional, visually appealing, and highly functional online presence that meets your specific goals and requirements.

CHAPTER FOUR: ADDING CONTENT AND MULTIMEDIA

Adding text and formatting

One of the most fundamental aspects of creating a website is adding text content. Whether it's for headings, paragraphs, or other textual elements, Wix provides a comprehensive set of tools to ensure that your content is visually appealing, easy to read, and well-formatted.

To add text to your Wix website, follow these steps:

1. **Select a Text Box:** In the Wix Editor, locate the "Text" element in the sidebar or the "Add" menu. Drag and drop a text box onto the desired location on your website canvas.

2. **Type or Paste Content:** Once the text box is placed, you can start typing or pasting your content directly into the box. Wix's text editor supports rich formatting options, allowing you to customize the appearance of your text.

3. **Formatting Options:** Wix offers a wide range of formatting options to enhance the readability and visual appeal of your text. These include font

selection, font size, text alignment, line spacing, and more. You can access these options through the text formatting toolbar or the settings panel.

4. **Headings and Structure**: To improve the structure and hierarchy of your content, utilize heading styles (H1, H2, H3, etc.). Headings not only organize your content but also aid in search engine optimization (SEO) and accessibility.

5. **Lists and Bullets**: For lists of items or steps, Wix provides tools to create ordered (numbered) or unordered (bulleted) lists. These can be particularly useful for instructions, product features, or any content that requires a structured list format.

6. **Links and Anchors**: Enhance the interactivity and navigation of your website by adding links to other pages or external resources. Wix also supports anchor links, which allow you to create smooth scrolling experiences within a single page.

7. **Styling and Customization**: While Wix offers default text styles, you can further customize the appearance of your text by adjusting colors, backgrounds, borders, and other styling options. This allows you to maintain consistency with your brand's visual identity.

Remember, well-formatted and visually appealing text not only enhances the user experience but also contributes to better readability and accessibility for your website visitors.

Inserting Images and Videos

Multimedia elements like images and videos can significantly enhance the visual appeal and engagement of your website. Wix provides a user-friendly interface for adding and managing these types of content, ensuring that your website stands out and effectively communicates your message.

Adding Images

1. **Upload Images**: In the Wix Editor, locate the "Media" or "Images" section in the sidebar or the "Add" menu. From here, you can upload images from your local device or connect to various cloud storage services like Google Drive or Dropbox.

2. **Drag and Drop**: Once your images are uploaded, you can easily drag and drop them onto the desired location on your website canvas.

3. **Image Settings**: Wix offers a range of settings and options for adjusting the appearance and behavior of your images. You can resize, crop, rotate, and add alt text (for accessibility and SEO purposes).

4. **Image Galleries**: If you have multiple images to showcase, Wix provides various gallery layouts and styles. These galleries allow you to display a collection of images in an organized and visually appealing manner.

Embedding Videos

1. **Video Sources**: Wix supports embedding videos from popular platforms like YouTube, Vimeo, and self-hosted video files. You can either upload your video directly or provide the URL of the video you

want to embed.

2. **Video Player**: Once your video is uploaded or the URL is provided, Wix will generate a video player that you can drag and drop onto your website canvas.

3. **Video Settings**: Customize the appearance and behavior of your video player by adjusting settings such as autoplay, loop, and aspect ratio. You can also add captions, annotations, and control the video's responsiveness across different devices.

4. **Video Backgrounds**: For a more immersive experience, Wix allows you to set videos as background elements on your website pages. This can create a dynamic and visually striking effect, perfect for landing pages or featured sections.

When working with images and videos, it's important to consider factors such as file size, resolution, and optimization to ensure optimal performance and fast loading times for your website visitors.

Working with Galleries

Galleries are a powerful way to showcase a collection of images, videos, or other multimedia content on your Wix website. Whether you're displaying a portfolio, product catalog, or a visual storytelling experience, Wix offers a variety of gallery layouts and customization options to suit your needs.

1. **Gallery Types**: Wix provides several gallery types to choose from, including grid layouts, sliders, masonry layouts, and more. Each gallery type offers a unique visual presentation and can be

tailored to fit your specific content and design requirements.

2. **Adding Media**: To populate your gallery, you can upload images or videos directly from your local device or connect to cloud storage services like Google Drive or Dropbox. Wix's intuitive interface makes it easy to manage and organize your media files.

3. **Gallery Settings**: Customize the appearance and behavior of your gallery by adjusting settings such as layout, spacing, transitions, navigation controls, and more. You can also add captions, titles, and descriptions to provide context and additional information for your media items.

4. **Lightbox and Zoom**: Wix's galleries often include a lightbox or zoom feature, allowing visitors to view larger versions of your images or videos by clicking or tapping on them. This enhances the viewing experience and provides a more immersive display of your content.

5. **Responsive Design**: Ensure that your galleries look great and function seamlessly across different devices and screen sizes. Wix's responsive design features automatically adjust the layout and presentation of your galleries based on the visitor's device.

6. **Integration with Other Features**: Galleries can be seamlessly integrated with other Wix features, such as e-commerce functionality (for product catalogs), blog posts (for visual storytelling), or portfolio pages (for showcasing your creative

work).

By leveraging Wix's gallery tools and customization options, you can create visually stunning and engaging displays that effectively showcase your content and enhance the overall user experience of your website.

Embedding third-party content

While Wix provides a wealth of built-in tools and features for adding content to your website, there may be times when you need to embed third-party content or integrate with external services. Fortunately, Wix offers various options to seamlessly incorporate these elements into your website.

1. **Embedding Code Snippets**: Wix allows you to embed code snippets from external sources, such as social media platforms, video hosting services, or interactive widgets. This can be particularly useful for adding social media feeds, video players, or custom functionality to your website.

2. **Integrating with Third-Party Apps**: Wix offers an extensive app market with a wide range of third-party integrations and applications. These apps can enhance your website's capabilities by adding features like forms, live chats, appointment booking systems, and more.

3. **Embedding Maps and Directions**: If your business has a physical location, you can embed interactive maps and directions directly on your website using Wix's built-in mapping tools or by integrating with services like Google Maps.

4. **Embedding Documents and Files**: For websites that require sharing documents or files, Wix

allows you to embed PDF files, Word documents, spreadsheets, and other file types directly onto your pages. This can be particularly useful for sharing reports, manuals, or other informational resources.

5. **Embedding Presentations and Slideshows**: If you need to showcase presentations or slideshows on your website, Wix supports embedding content from platforms like SlideShare or PowerPoint. This can be a valuable feature for businesses, educators, or anyone looking to share visual content in an engaging and interactive format.

When embedding third-party content, it's important to ensure that you have the necessary permissions and follow any applicable guidelines or terms of service. Additionally, consider the potential impact on website performance and load times, as embedded content may require additional resources to load and display properly.

Optimizing content for SEO

In today's digital landscape, having a website is just the first step. To ensure that your website is discoverable and ranks well in search engine results, it's crucial to optimize your content for search engine optimization (SEO). Wix provides a range of tools and settings to help you improve your website's visibility and attract more organic traffic.

1. **Page Titles and Descriptions**: Each page on your Wix website should have a unique and descriptive title and meta description. These elements not only help search engines understand the content of your pages but also appear in search results, influencing whether users click through to your

site.

2. **Keyword Research and Integration**: Identify relevant keywords and phrases that your target audience is likely to search for. Strategically incorporate these keywords into your page titles, headings, body content, and meta descriptions. However, be cautious of keyword stuffing, as this can negatively impact your SEO efforts and user experience.

3. **Alt Text for Images**: Search engines cannot inherently understand the content of images, but they can read the alt text (alternative text) associated with them. Ensure that you provide descriptive and relevant alt text for all images on your website, as this can improve your SEO and accessibility.

4. **Internal and External Linking**: A well-structured internal linking strategy can help search engines better understand the hierarchy and relationships between pages on your website. Additionally, incorporating relevant external links to authoritative sources can enhance your site's credibility and authority.

5. **Mobile Optimization**: With the increasing number of users accessing the internet from mobile devices, it's crucial to ensure that your website is mobile-friendly. Wix's responsive design features can help you create a seamless mobile experience, which is a ranking factor for search engines.

6. **Site Structure and Navigation**: A logical and

user-friendly site structure and navigation can improve the overall user experience and make it easier for search engines to crawl and index your content effectively.

7. **Page Load Speed**: Search engines prioritize websites that load quickly, as this enhances the user experience. Wix provides tools and recommendations to optimize your website's performance, such as image compression and code minification.

8. **Sitemaps and Robots**.txt: Wix allows you to generate and submit sitemaps to search engines, making it easier for them to discover and crawl your website's content. Additionally, you can configure a robots.txt file to specify which pages or directories should be crawled or excluded by search engine bots.

9. **Analytics and Tracking**: Integrate your website with analytics tools like Google Analytics to monitor your website's performance, track user behavior, and identify areas for improvement in terms of SEO and user experience.

10. **Staying Updated**: SEO best practices and algorithms are constantly evolving. Stay informed about the latest trends and updates in the SEO landscape, and adjust your strategies accordingly to maintain and improve your website's search engine visibility.

By following these SEO best practices and leveraging Wix's built-in tools and features, you can optimize your website's content and structure for better search engine visibility, driving more organic traffic to your online presence.

CHAPTER FIVE: ADVANCED DESIGN AND CUSTOMIZATION

Customizing the Header and Footer

The header and footer sections of a website play crucial roles in establishing a cohesive and professional online presence. The header typically includes elements such as the logo, primary navigation menu, and other essential links, while the footer often contains additional navigation, contact information, and legal disclaimers. Wix provides a range of customization options to ensure that these sections align seamlessly with your brand's identity and website's design.

Customizing the header:

1. **Logo and Branding**: The header is the perfect place to prominently display your brand's logo. Wix allows you to easily upload and adjust the size and positioning of your logo, ensuring it's visible and aligns with your brand guidelines.

2. **Navigation Menu**: The primary navigation menu

is typically located in the header, providing visitors with easy access to your website's main sections and pages. Wix offers various menu styles, including horizontal, vertical, and dropdown menus, allowing you to choose the layout that best suits your design and user experience goals.

3. **Additional Elements**: Beyond the logo and navigation menu, you can further enhance your header by incorporating additional elements such as search bars, call-to-action buttons, social media icons, or promotional banners. These elements can help draw attention to important features or encourage specific actions from your visitors.

4. **Sticky Headers**: For an improved user experience, Wix enables you to create "sticky" headers that remain visible as visitors scroll down the page. This ensures that your logo, navigation menu, and other essential elements are always accessible, regardless of where the visitor is on your website.

Customizing the Footer:

1. **Secondary Navigation**: The footer is an ideal location to include a secondary navigation menu, providing additional links to important pages or resources that may not be part of your primary navigation.

2. **Contact Information**: Use the footer to prominently display your business's contact information, such as address, phone number, email address, and social media links. This ensures that visitors can easily find and connect

with you, regardless of which page they're on.

3. **Legal Information**: The footer is also a common place to include legal information, such as copyright notices, terms of service, privacy policies, and disclaimers. Wix allows you to easily add and format this content, ensuring compliance with legal requirements.

4. **Consistent Branding**: Just like the header, the footer should reflect your brand's visual identity. Incorporate your brand's colors, fonts, and design elements to maintain a cohesive look and feel throughout your website.

5. **Customizable Layout**: Wix provides various layout options for the footer, allowing you to organize and present information in a way that best suits your website's design and content. You can choose from single-row or multi-row layouts, adjust spacing, and even add background images or patterns.

By customizing the header and footer sections of your Wix website, you can create a professional and visually appealing online presence that reinforces your brand, improves navigation, and provides essential information to your visitors.

Creating forms and surveys

Forms and surveys are powerful tools for gathering valuable information from your website visitors, whether it's collecting leads, conducting market research, or soliciting feedback. Wix offers a comprehensive suite of form-building capabilities, allowing you to create custom forms and surveys tailored to your specific needs.

1. **Form Builder**: Wix's intuitive form builder makes it easy to create various types of forms, including contact forms, registration forms, order forms, and surveys. You can drag and drop different field types, such as text inputs, drop-down menus, checkboxes, and radio buttons, to design your form.

2. **Field Customization**: Customize each form field to match your brand's visual identity by adjusting colors, fonts, and styles. Additionally, you can add validation rules, placeholders, and instructions to ensure that your visitors provide accurate and complete information.

3. **Form Logic**: Enhance the user experience and streamline data collection by incorporating form logic. This feature allows you to conditionally display or hide specific fields based on the visitor's responses, creating a more personalized and relevant experience.

4. **Multi-Step Forms**: For longer or more complex forms, Wix enables you to create multi-step forms, breaking the process into manageable sections. This can improve completion rates and provide a more user-friendly experience for your visitors.

5. **Form Submissions and Notifications**: Once a visitor submits a form, Wix provides various options for handling the data. You can receive email notifications, export submissions to a spreadsheet, or integrate with third-party applications for advanced data management and

analysis.

6. **CAPTCHA and Spam Protection**: To prevent spam and bot submissions, Wix offers CAPTCHA and other spam protection measures, ensuring that your forms are secure and only legitimate submissions are recorded.

7. **Responsive Design**: Like all elements of your Wix website, forms and surveys are fully responsive, ensuring a seamless experience across desktop, tablet, and mobile devices.

By leveraging Wix's form and survey capabilities, you can gather valuable insights, engage with your audience, and streamline data collection processes, ultimately improving your ability to make informed decisions and provide better services or products.

Adding Animations and Effects

While content and functionality are essential components of a successful website, incorporating visually appealing animations and effects can elevate the user experience and leave a lasting impression on your visitors. Wix offers a range of tools and features to help you add dynamic and engaging animations to your website, bringing your design to life.

1. **Entrance Animations**: Capture your visitors' attention by adding entrance animations to various elements on your website. These animations trigger when an element comes into view, creating a smooth and visually appealing transition. Wix provides a variety of entrance animation options, such as fade-in, slide-in, and zoom effects.

2. **Scroll Animations**: As visitors scroll through your website, you can incorporate animations that respond to their scrolling behavior. Wix offers scroll-based animations that can reveal or highlight content, create parallax effects, or trigger other interactive elements.

3. **Hover Animations**: Enhance the interactivity of your website by adding hover animations to buttons, links, images, or other clickable elements. These animations can provide subtle visual feedback, guiding visitors and encouraging them to explore your website further.

4. **Transition Animations**: Create a seamless and cohesive experience by incorporating transition animations between page loads or when navigating from one section to another. Wix's transition animations can help maintain a sense of continuity and provide a polished, professional look and feel.

5. **Background Animations**: Bring your website's background to life with animated backgrounds, such as subtle particle effects, parallax scrolling, or video backgrounds. These animations can add depth and movement to your design, creating a more engaging and immersive experience for your visitors.

6. **Animation Settings**: Wix provides extensive customization options for animations, allowing you to adjust the duration, delay, easing, and looping behavior to achieve the desired effect. You can also control animation triggers, such as scroll

position, hover events, or manual triggers.

7. **Performance Optimization**: While animations can enhance the visual appeal of your website, it's important to strike a balance between aesthetics and performance. Wix offers optimization tools and guidelines to ensure that your animations load quickly and don't negatively impact the user experience.

By strategically incorporating animations and effects throughout your Wix website, you can create a dynamic and visually captivating online presence that engages your visitors, reinforces your brand's personality, and leaves a lasting impression.

Integrating social media

In today's digital landscape, social media plays a pivotal role in building brand awareness, fostering community engagement, and driving traffic to your website. Wix recognizes the importance of social media integration and provides a range of tools and features to seamlessly incorporate social media elements into your website.

1. **Social Media Icons and Links**: One of the most common ways to integrate social media on your Wix website is by adding icons and links to your various social media profiles. These can be added to the header, footer, or any other section of your website, making it easy for visitors to connect with you on their preferred social platforms.

2. **Social Media Feeds**: Wix allows you to embed live social media feeds directly onto your website pages. Whether it's displaying your latest Twitter updates, showcasing your Instagram posts, or

featuring customer reviews from Facebook, social media feeds can add dynamic and engaging content to your site.

3. **Social Sharing Buttons**: Encourage visitors to share your content by adding social sharing buttons to your blog posts, product pages, or other relevant sections. Wix provides seamless integration with popular social networks, making it easy for visitors to share your content with their own networks and potentially drive more traffic to your website.

4. **Social Login and Registration**: Simplify the registration and login process for your visitors by offering social login options. Wix integrates with popular social media platforms, allowing users to sign up or log in using their existing social media credentials, enhancing convenience and reducing friction.

5. **Social Advertising and Tracking**: For businesses leveraging social media advertising, Wix provides powerful tools to create, manage, and track campaigns across various platforms. With seamless integration and robust analytics, you can maximize the impact of your social media marketing efforts.

6. **Creating Social Media Ads**: Wix's advertising platform allows you to create visually appealing and targeted social media ads with ease. Whether you're promoting a product, service, or event, you can design captivating ad creatives directly within the Wix interface. Customize

the ad's layout, imagery, text, and call-to-action buttons to align with your brand's identity and campaign objectives. Wix supports ad creation for popular platforms like Facebook, Instagram, and Google, ensuring that your ads reach the right audience across multiple channels. You can also leverage Wix's built-in targeting options to refine your audience based on demographics, interests, behaviors, and locations, increasing the likelihood of engagement and conversions.

7. **Ad Campaign Management**: Once your social media ads are created, Wix provides a centralized dashboard for managing and monitoring your campaigns. From this dashboard, you can easily launch new campaigns, adjust budgets, and track performance metrics in real-time. The dashboard also offers insight into important metrics such as impressions, clicks, conversions, and cost per acquisition (CPA). This data-driven approach allows you to identify which ads and targeting strategies are performing well and make informed decisions about optimizing your campaigns for better results.

8. **Retargeting and Lookalike Audiences**: Wix's advertising tools also support retargeting and lookalike audience targeting, powerful strategies for reaching potential customers who have already shown interest in your brand or share similar characteristics with your existing customer base. With retargeting, you can create ads specifically tailored to users who have previously visited your website or interacted

with your social media profiles. This approach helps to nurture leads and encourage conversions by keeping your brand top-of-mind. Lookalike audience targeting, on the other hand, leverages machine learning algorithms to identify new potential customers who share similar traits and behaviors with your existing customer base. This technique allows you to expand your reach and acquire new customers with a higher likelihood of engagement and conversion.

9. **Tracking and Analytics**: Wix provides comprehensive tracking and analytics capabilities to measure the success of your social media advertising campaigns. You can track key performance indicators (KPIs) such as website traffic, lead generation, and sales and attribute them directly to your social media ad campaigns. The platform integrates with popular analytics tools like Google Analytics, allowing you to gain deeper insights into user behavior, audience demographics, and conversion paths. This data-driven approach empowers you to make informed decisions about optimizing your campaigns, refining your targeting strategies, and allocating your advertising budget effectively. By leveraging Wix's social advertising and tracking features, businesses can streamline their social media marketing efforts, reach highly targeted audiences, and measure the impact of their campaigns with precision. This comprehensive approach helps drive brand awareness, engagement, and ultimately, conversions and revenue growth.

CHAPTER SIX: E-COMMERCE AND ONLINE SELLING

Setting up an online store

Establishing an online store has become a crucial component for businesses of all sizes, allowing them to reach a wider audience and capitalize on the growing e-commerce market. Wix's powerful e-commerce platform simplifies the process of creating and managing an online store, making it accessible even for those without technical expertise.

Begin by choosing a suitable online store template that aligns with your brand's identity and desired aesthetic. Wix offers a diverse selection of professionally designed templates, each tailored to different industries and product categories. Alternatively, you can start from scratch and build a customized store that reflects your unique vision.

Once you've selected a template, it's time to populate your store with products. Wix's intuitive interface allows you to easily add product descriptions, images, pricing, and other relevant details. You can organize your products into categories and subcategories, ensuring a seamless browsing experience for your customers.

To enhance the visual appeal of your online store, consider incorporating high-quality product photography and videos. Wix provides tools for image optimization, ensuring that your products are displayed in their best light without compromising loading times.

Managing products and inventory

As your online store grows, efficient product and inventory management become crucial. Wix's e-commerce platform offers robust tools to streamline these processes, saving you time and reducing the risk of errors.

Utilize Wix's inventory management system to track stock levels, set low-stock alerts, and automatically update product availability on your website. This feature ensures that customers are never presented with out-of-stock items, minimizing frustration and enhancing the overall shopping experience.

For businesses with multiple product variations, such as different sizes, colors, or materials, Wix allows you to create and manage these options seamlessly. Customers can easily select their preferred combinations, ensuring accurate ordering and fulfillment.

Additionally, Wix provides tools for bulk product imports and exports, enabling you to efficiently manage large product catalogs or integrate with third-party inventory management systems.

Configuring Payment Gateways

Offering secure and convenient payment options is essential for building trust with your customers and ensuring a smooth checkout process. Wix integrates with various popular payment gateways, including PayPal, Stripe, and Square, allowing you to accept a wide range of payment methods, such as credit cards, debit cards, and digital wallets.

During the setup process, you'll be guided through the necessary steps to connect your preferred payment gateway to your online store. Wix's user-friendly interface simplifies the configuration, ensuring that your customers can complete their purchases with confidence.

To further enhance security and protect your customers' sensitive information, Wix offers advanced fraud protection features. These include address verification, CVV checks, and secure data encryption, helping to minimize the risk of unauthorized transactions and chargebacks.

Handling shipping and taxes

Efficient shipping and tax management are crucial components of a successful online store. Wix provides comprehensive tools to streamline these processes, ensuring a hassle-free experience for both you and your customers.

Start by configuring your shipping options, such as flat rates, real-time carrier rates, or custom calculations based on weight or destination. Wix's integration with major shipping carriers like USPS, FedEx, and UPS allows you to provide accurate shipping estimates and tracking information to your customers.

For businesses operating in multiple tax jurisdictions, Wix's tax management features can significantly simplify the process. Set up tax rates based on your customers' locations, ensuring that the correct taxes are automatically applied during checkout. This feature helps you remain compliant with local tax regulations and provides transparency to your customers.

Additionally, Wix offers tools for printing shipping labels, packing slips, and invoices, streamlining the fulfillment process and ensuring a professional and organized approach to order management.

Promoting and marketing your store

Launching an online store is just the first step; effective promotion and marketing strategies are essential to drive traffic, increase sales, and build a loyal customer base. Wix provides various tools and integrations to help you market your store effectively.

Leverage Wix's built-in search engine optimization (SEO) features to optimize your online store for better visibility in search engine results. This includes optimizing product descriptions, titles, and meta tags, as well as implementing structured data markup to enhance your store's appearance in rich search results.

Integrate your online store with social media platforms like Facebook, Instagram, and Twitter to expand your reach and engage with potential customers. Share product updates, promotions, and behind-the-scenes content to build a strong brand presence and foster customer loyalty.

Wix also offers email marketing tools, allowing you to create targeted campaigns, newsletters, and automated email sequences. Use these features to nurture leads, announce new products, and incentivize repeat purchases through exclusive offers and discounts.

Additionally, consider leveraging Wix's integration with third-party advertising platforms like Google Ads and Facebook Ads. These integrations enable you to create and manage targeted advertising campaigns directly from within the Wix platform, driving qualified traffic to your online store.

By combining Wix's powerful e-commerce features with effective promotion and marketing strategies, you can establish a thriving online presence, attract new customers, and foster long-lasting relationships with your existing customer base.

CHAPTER SEVEN: ANALYTICS AND TRACKING

Understanding Website Analytics

In the digital age, data-driven decision-making is crucial for the success of any online venture. Website analytics provide invaluable insights into your audience's behavior, preferences, and interactions with your site. By understanding these metrics, you can make informed decisions to optimize your website's performance, enhance the user experience, and ultimately drive more conversions.

At the core of website analytics lies the ability to track and analyze various key performance indicators (KPIs). These metrics can include visitor numbers, page views, bounce rates, traffic sources, and conversion rates, among others. Each KPI offers valuable insights into different aspects of your website's performance and user engagement.

For example, tracking visitor numbers and page views can help you gauge the overall popularity and reach of your website, while bounce rates and average session duration provide insights into how engaging and user-friendly your content is. Traffic source data can reveal which marketing channels are most effective in driving visitors to your site, enabling you to allocate your resources accordingly.

Integrating analytics tools

To effectively leverage the power of website analytics, it is essential to integrate robust analytics tools into your Wix website. Wix offers seamless integration with industry-leading platforms like Google Analytics, enabling you to access a wealth of data and insights.

Setting up Google Analytics with your Wix website is a straightforward process. First, you'll need to create a Google Analytics account and obtain a unique tracking code. Wix provides a dedicated section in the website settings where you can easily paste this code, allowing Google Analytics to begin collecting data from your site.

Once integrated, Google Analytics will provide you with a comprehensive dashboard displaying various metrics and visualizations. You can customize these reports to focus on the KPIs most relevant to your business goals, allowing for more targeted analysis and decision-making.

Tracking visitor behavior

While quantitative metrics like page views and bounce rates are valuable, understanding visitor behavior on a deeper level can unlock even more insights. Website analytics tools offer advanced features that allow you to track and analyze visitor behavior, such as heat maps, session recordings, and user flow visualizations.

Heat maps provide a visual representation of where visitors are clicking, scrolling, and engaging with your website's content. This information can help you identify areas that may require design or layout adjustments to improve the user experience and conversions.

Session recordings, on the other hand, capture actual visitor interactions with your website, allowing you to observe their journey and identify potential pain points or areas for improvement. User flow visualizations offer a bird's-eye view of the paths visitors take through your website, helping you optimize navigation and content structure.

Analyzing website performance

Analyzing website performance is an ongoing process that involves monitoring key metrics over time and identifying trends or patterns. By regularly reviewing your analytics data, you can quickly identify areas that require attention or optimization.

For instance, if you notice a sudden spike or drop in traffic, you can investigate the potential causes, such as changes in your marketing strategies, seasonality, or external factors like algorithm updates or industry trends. By understanding the root causes, you can make informed decisions to address the issue or capitalize on the opportunity.

Additionally, website analytics can help you assess the performance of specific pages, products, or campaigns. By tracking metrics like conversion rates, revenue generated, and average order value, you can determine which elements of your website are driving the most success and which areas may need improvement.

Optimizing for Better Results

The true power of website analytics lies in its ability to inform data-driven optimizations and improvements. Armed with insights from your analytics data, you can make strategic decisions to enhance various aspects of your website, ultimately leading to better results and increased conversions.

For example, if your analytics reveal that a particular product page has a high bounce rate, you may consider optimizing the page's content, layout, or call-to-action to improve engagement and conversions. Similarly, if you notice that a specific traffic source is driving a high volume of low-quality visitors, you can adjust your marketing strategies or targeting criteria to attract more relevant and engaged audiences.

Additionally, website analytics can guide your content creation and SEO efforts. By analyzing which types of content resonate best with your audience and which keywords drive the most traffic, you can tailor your content strategy to better meet the needs and interests of your target audience.

Continuous monitoring, testing, and optimization based on your analytics data will not only improve your website's performance but also contribute to a better overall user experience, fostering customer loyalty and driving long-term success.

CHAPTER EIGHT: PUBLISHING AND MAINTENANCE

Previewing and Testing Your Website

Before publishing your website to the world, it's essential to thoroughly preview and test it to ensure a seamless and professional experience for your visitors. Wix provides powerful tools to help you identify and resolve any potential issues, ensuring that your website is ready for launch.

Start by using Wix's built-in preview mode, which allows you to view your website as it would appear to visitors. This mode offers various viewing options, including desktop, tablet, and mobile views, enabling you to ensure consistent and responsive design across different devices and screen sizes.

During the preview process, pay close attention to every aspect of your website, from the navigation menus and layout to the content and functionality. Test all links, forms, and interactive elements to ensure they work as intended. Additionally, check for any spelling or grammar errors, broken images, or formatting issues that may detract from the overall user experience.

Once you've thoroughly reviewed your website in preview mode, consider conducting user testing with a small group of individuals who represent your target audience. Gather feedback on usability, design, and overall impressions, and use this valuable input to make any necessary adjustments before publishing.

Connecting a Domain

To establish a professional online presence, it's crucial to secure a unique domain name for your website. Wix offers seamless domain registration and management, allowing you to easily connect your desired domain to your website.

During the website creation process, Wix will prompt you to search for and purchase an available domain name. Alternatively, you can transfer an existing domain you own to your Wix account. The platform provides step-by-step guidance to ensure a smooth domain connection process.

Once your domain is connected, Wix automatically configures the necessary DNS settings, ensuring that visitors can access your website by typing your domain name into their web browsers. This streamlined process eliminates the need for technical expertise, making it accessible for users of all skill levels.

Publishing your website

After previewing, testing, and connecting your domain, it's time to publish your website and make it live on the internet. Wix offers a straightforward publishing process, ensuring that your website is accessible to visitors worldwide.

Before publishing, Wix will prompt you to review your website one final time and make any necessary adjustments. Once you're satisfied with your website's appearance and functionality, simply click the "Publish" button, and Wix will handle the rest.

During the publishing process, Wix optimizes your website's files for efficient delivery and ensures compatibility with various web browsers and devices. This optimization helps to provide a smooth and consistent experience for your visitors, regardless of their device or browser.

Once your website is published, Wix provides a unique URL that you can share with others, allowing them to access and explore your online presence. Additionally, if you've connected a custom domain, visitors can now access your website by typing your domain name into their web browsers.

Maintaining and updating your website
A website is never truly complete; it's an ongoing project that requires regular maintenance and updates to keep it fresh, relevant, and engaging for your visitors. Wix offers a user-friendly content management system (CMS) that simplifies the process of making updates and modifications to your website.

Whenever you need to make changes to your website's content, design, or functionality, simply log into your Wix account and access the website editor. From here, you can modify existing pages, add new ones, update text, images, and multimedia content, and even add or remove features and functionalities.

Wix also provides tools for managing comments, form submissions, and other user-generated content, ensuring that your website remains up-to-date and responsive to your visitors' interactions.

Regularly updating your website with fresh content, such as blog posts, news articles, or product listings, can help improve your search engine rankings and keep your visitors engaged. Additionally, staying up-to-date with the latest design trends and user experience best practices can help enhance the overall appeal and usability of your website.

Backing Up and Restoring Your Site

Despite your best efforts, unexpected events or technical issues may occur, potentially compromising your website's integrity or data. To safeguard your hard work and ensure business continuity, it's crucial to regularly back up your website and have a reliable method for restoring it when needed.

Wix offers built-in backup and restore functionality, making it easy to create and manage backups of your entire website, including all content, design elements, and settings. You can schedule automatic backups to occur at regular intervals or manually create backups whenever necessary.

In the event of data loss, corruption, or any other issue that requires restoring your website, Wix's restore feature allows you to quickly and easily revert to a previous backup. This process can help minimize downtime and ensure that your website remains accessible and functional for your visitors.

Additionally, Wix provides version control for your website, allowing you to track and revert changes made to specific pages or elements. This feature can be particularly useful when collaborating with team members or making significant updates, as it allows you to easily undo unwanted modifications or compare different versions of your website.

By prioritizing regular backups and taking advantage of Wix's robust restore capabilities, you can safeguard your website against potential threats and ensure business continuity, giving you peace of mind and allowing you to focus on growing your online presence.

CHAPTER NINE: ADVANCED FEATURES AND INTEGRATIONS

Adding third-party apps and plugins

While Wix offers a comprehensive suite of features and tools, there may be instances where you require additional functionality or specialized integrations to enhance your website's capabilities. Fortunately, Wix's App Market provides access to a vast array of third-party apps and plugins, enabling you to extend the platform's functionality and tailor it to your specific needs.

The App Market is a curated collection of applications developed by Wix's partners and the broader developer community. These apps cover a wide range of categories, including marketing, analytics, e-commerce, communication, and productivity tools, among others.

To add an app or plugin to your Wix website, simply browse the App Market and explore the available options. Each app listing provides detailed information about its features, compatibility, and pricing (if applicable). Once you've found an app that meets your requirements, follow the straightforward installation process, and Wix will seamlessly integrate the app into your website.

Some popular third-party apps and plugins that can enhance your Wix website include:

1. **E-commerce extensions**: These apps can add advanced features like product reviews, wish lists, and inventory management to your online store.

2. **Social media integrations**: apps that allow you to embed social media feeds, display social sharing buttons, and leverage social login functionality.

3. **Marketing tools**: plugins for email marketing, lead generation, and customer relationship management (CRM) integration.

4. **Analytics and tracking**: Advanced analytics tools for in-depth website performance analysis and visitor behavior tracking.

5. **Multimedia enhancements**: apps that enable you to add videos, music players, or even virtual reality (VR) experiences to your website.

Remember, when adding third-party apps and plugins, it's essential to review their compatibility, security, and privacy policies to ensure they align with your website's requirements and comply with relevant regulations.

Integrating with CRM and marketing tools

In today's data-driven business landscape, integrating your website with customer relationship management (CRM) and marketing tools can streamline your processes, enhance customer engagement, and ultimately drive growth for your business.

Wix offers seamless integration with popular CRM platforms like HubSpot, Salesforce, and Zoho, allowing you to capture and manage leads generated from your website. By connecting your website's forms and contact information to your CRM system, you can automatically populate customer data, track interactions, and follow up with leads more efficiently.

Additionally, Wix provides integration options with marketing automation tools like MailChimp, Constant Contact, and ActiveCampaign. These integrations enable you to create targeted email campaigns, capture subscriber information from your website, and nurture leads through automated email sequences and personalized content.

Integrating your Wix website with these powerful tools can greatly enhance your marketing efforts and customer relationship management strategies. For example, you can:

1. **Segment your audience**: Collect and analyze visitor data from your website to create targeted segments for more personalized marketing campaigns.

2. **Automate lead nurturing**: Set up automated email sequences triggered by specific actions or behaviors on your website, such as form submissions or product purchases.

3. **Retarget visitors**: Use visitor data from your website to create retargeting campaigns and reach potential customers across various platforms.

4. **Analyze customer journeys**: Track customer interactions and behaviors on your website to gain insights into their preferences and pain points, allowing you to optimize the customer

experience.

By leveraging these integrations, you can streamline your sales and marketing processes, foster better customer relationships, and ultimately drive more conversions and revenue for your business.

Creating multilingual websites

In our increasingly globalized world, businesses often need to cater to audiences from diverse linguistic backgrounds. Wix recognizes this need and provides powerful tools to create multilingual websites, enabling you to reach a wider audience and enhance your online presence.

Wix's multilingual capabilities allow you to create and manage multiple language versions of your website from a single dashboard. You can easily add new languages, translate content, and toggle between different language versions with just a few clicks.

To create a multilingual website, begin by enabling the multilingual feature in your Wix account settings. Once enabled, you can add new languages and select the default language for your website. Wix will then provide you with a dedicated interface for managing and translating your content across all added languages.

You have the flexibility to translate your website's content manually or leverage Wix's built-in machine translation integration with services like Google Translate. While machine translation can be a convenient starting point, it's recommended to review and refine the translations to ensure accuracy and cultural relevance.

In addition to translating text content, Wix's multilingual capabilities extend to various website elements, including menus, buttons, forms, and even e-commerce product descriptions. This comprehensive approach ensures a consistent and seamless experience for visitors, regardless of their preferred language.

To further enhance the multilingual experience, Wix offers language-specific SEO options, allowing you to optimize your website's content and metadata for better visibility in search engine results across different languages and regions.

By creating a multilingual website, you can expand your reach, build trust with a global audience, and ultimately increase your website's potential for success in the international market.

Implementing security features

Ensuring the security and privacy of your website and its visitors is of paramount importance, especially in today's digital landscape where cyber threats are constantly evolving. Wix offers a range of robust security features to help protect your website and safeguard sensitive data.

One of the fundamental security measures provided by Wix is secure encryption using SSL/TLS protocols. This encryption ensures that all data transmitted between your website and visitors' browsers is securely encrypted, preventing unauthorized access and protecting sensitive information such as login credentials and payment details.

Wix also implements regular security updates and patches to address any vulnerabilities or security threats that may arise. This proactive approach helps to maintain the integrity and security of the Wix platform, ensuring that your website remains protected against potential attacks or breaches.

In addition to these foundational security measures, Wix

offers advanced features to further enhance your website's security, including:

1. **Two-factor authentication**: Add an extra layer of security by requiring a secondary form of authentication, such as a one-time code sent to your mobile device, when logging into your Wix account or making significant changes to your website.

2. **Password protection**: Protect specific pages or sections of your website with password protection, allowing access only to authorized users.

3. **Visitor data protection**: Implement measures to safeguard visitor data, such as form submissions and personal information, ensuring compliance with data privacy regulations like GDPR.

4. **Malware and spam protection**: Wix employs advanced techniques to detect and prevent malware infections and spam on your website, ensuring a safe browsing experience for your visitors.

By leveraging these security features, you can significantly reduce the risk of security breaches, protect sensitive data, and foster trust among your website visitors, ultimately contributing to the long-term success and credibility of your online presence.

Utilizing Developer Tools

While Wix's user-friendly interface and comprehensive features cater to a wide range of users, some advanced users or developers may require additional customization options and deeper control over their website's functionality. To address these needs, Wix provides a suite of developer tools and resources.

One of the key developer tools offered by Wix is the Velo platform, which allows developers to create custom web applications and integrate them seamlessly with Wix websites. Velo provides a robust development environment with support for server-side logic, data management, and integration with external APIs and services.

Using Velo, developers can build custom functionality tailored to specific business requirements, such as complex e-commerce solutions, advanced form processing, or data-driven applications. Additionally, Velo supports the creation of headless websites, enabling developers to separate the front-end and back-end components, allowing for greater flexibility and integration with other systems or frameworks.

For developers who prefer to work with code directly, Wix offers the Wix Code platform. Wix Code allows developers to write and customize their website's functionality using JavaScript, React, and other modern web development technologies. This platform provides access to Wix's robust APIs, enabling developers to integrate third-party services, create custom widgets, and extend the platform's capabilities.

Furthermore, Wix provides comprehensive documentation, developer forums, and code samples to support the developer community. These resources help developers learn and navigate the platform's features, troubleshoot issues, and collaborate with other developers to solve complex challenges.

By leveraging Wix's developer tools and resources,

advanced users and developers can unlock the full potential of the platform, creating highly customized and sophisticated websites that meet even the most demanding requirements.

CHAPTER TEN: TROUBLESHOOTING AND SUPPORT

Common Issues and Solutions

Even with the most user-friendly platform, you may encounter issues or challenges while building and maintaining your website. Understanding common problems and their solutions can help you resolve them quickly and efficiently, minimizing downtime and ensuring a smooth user experience.

One common issue faced by many website owners is slow page loading times. This can be caused by various factors, such as large image file sizes, excessive third-party scripts, or hosting-related performance bottlenecks. To address this, optimize your images by compressing them without sacrificing quality, minify your code, and consider upgrading your hosting plan or utilizing a content delivery network (CDN).

Another frequent challenge is compatibility issues across different web browsers and devices. While modern web technologies have improved cross-browser compatibility, some legacy browsers or older device models may still experience rendering or functionality issues. To mitigate this, regularly test your website on various browsers and devices, and consider implementing responsive design techniques or progressive enhancement strategies.

User authentication and security-related issues are also common concerns. Ensure that your website is equipped with robust security measures, such as SSL/TLS encryption, strong password policies, and two-factor authentication. Additionally, stay informed about the latest security vulnerabilities and promptly apply any necessary updates or patches.

If you encounter issues related to specific features or functionalities, consult the platform's documentation or knowledge base for troubleshooting guides and solutions. Many common problems have already been addressed, and following the recommended steps can often resolve the issue efficiently.

Utilizing Wix Support Resources

When faced with challenges or questions that you can't resolve on your own, it's essential to leverage the support resources provided by the website platform. Most reputable platforms offer a variety of support channels to assist users and ensure their success.

One of the primary support resources is typically a comprehensive knowledge base or documentation center. These resources often contain detailed articles, tutorials, and troubleshooting guides covering a wide range of topics, from getting started with the platform to advanced features and best practices.

In addition to self-service resources, many platforms offer direct support channels, such as email support, live chat, or phone support. These channels allow you to connect with knowledgeable support representatives who can provide personalized assistance and guidance tailored to your specific needs.

Some platforms also maintain active user communities or forums where you can interact with other users, ask questions, share insights, and collaborate on solutions. These communities can be invaluable resources, as they often contain a wealth of collective knowledge and real-world experiences from users with diverse backgrounds and expertise.

When seeking support, it's essential to provide clear and detailed information about your issue or question. This may include screenshots, error messages, or step-by-step descriptions of the actions you've taken. The more information you can provide, the easier it will be for support representatives or community members to understand and address your concern effectively.

Building a support network

While leveraging the platform's official support resources is crucial, building a personal support network can also be beneficial for website owners and developers. This network can consist of fellow users, industry professionals, and subject matter experts who can offer guidance, insights, and collaborative problem-solving.

One way to build a support network is by participating in local or online communities related to web development, design, or your specific industry. Attend meetups, join online forums, or participate in social media groups where you can connect with like-minded individuals and share knowledge and experiences.

Another approach is to seek out mentors or experienced

professionals who can provide guidance and advice based on their expertise. This could involve reaching out to successful website owners or developers in your industry, attending workshops or webinars, or even hiring a consultant for focused guidance and support.

Building a support network not only provides access to valuable resources and knowledge but also fosters collaboration and networking opportunities. By engaging with others in your field, you can stay up-to-date with industry trends, best practices, and emerging technologies, which can inform your website development and maintenance strategies.

Best Practices for Website Maintenance

Maintaining a successful website requires a proactive approach and adherence to best practices. By implementing these practices, you can ensure that your website remains secure, up-to-date, and optimized for performance and user experience.

Regular software updates and security patches: Stay vigilant about applying updates and security patches to your website platform, plugins, and any third-party integrations. These updates often address vulnerabilities, introduce new features, and improve performance and compatibility.

Backup and restore strategies: Implement a robust backup strategy to safeguard your website's data, content, and configurations. Schedule regular backups and store them securely off-site or in the cloud. Periodically test your restore process to ensure its reliability in case of data loss or system failure.

Performance monitoring and optimization: Continuously

monitor your website's performance using analytics tools and user feedback. Identify and address any performance bottlenecks, such as slow-loading pages, server response times, or resource-intensive processes. Optimize your website's code, assets, and server configurations for optimal performance.

Content management and organization: Establish a content strategy and maintain a well-organized content structure. Regularly review and update your website's content to ensure accuracy, relevance, and consistency with your brand and messaging.

User experience (UX) testing and improvements: Gather feedback from your users through surveys, usability testing, or analytics data. Use this information to identify areas for improvement in navigation, layout, accessibility, and the overall user experience. Continuously iterate and refine your website based on user insights.

By adhering to these best practices, you can prolong the lifespan of your website, improve its overall quality, and provide a consistent and enjoyable experience for your users.

Future trends and updates

The web development landscape is constantly evolving, with new technologies, trends, and best practices emerging regularly. Staying informed about these advancements can help you future-proof your website and ensure that it remains competitive and engaging for your target audience.

One notable trend is the increasing emphasis on mobile-first design and development. As more users access the internet through smartphones and tablets, it's crucial to optimize your website for seamless mobile experiences. This may involve adopting responsive design techniques, leveraging progressive web app (PWA) technologies, or implementing accelerated mobile pages (AMP) for faster loading times.

Accessibility and inclusivity are also becoming increasingly important factors in web development. Ensuring that your website is accessible to users with disabilities or special needs not only expands your potential audience but also aligns with legal requirements and best practices. This may involve implementing accessibility features such as screen reader compatibility, keyboard navigation, and color contrast optimization.

The integration of artificial intelligence (AI) and machine learning (ML) technologies is another emerging trend that can enhance website functionality and user experiences. AI-powered chatbots, personalized content recommendations, and predictive analytics are just a few examples of how these technologies can be leveraged to improve user engagement and conversions.

Additionally, keeping an eye on updates and new features released by your website platform can provide opportunities for enhancing your website's capabilities and staying ahead of the curve. Regularly review the platform's roadmap, release notes, and community forums to stay informed about upcoming changes and plan for potential upgrades or migrations.

By staying abreast of future trends and updates, you can ensure that your website remains relevant, engaging, and competitive in an ever-evolving digital landscape.

CONCLUSION

Throughout this comprehensive handbook, we have explored the powerful features and capabilities of the Wix website builder. From setting up your account and creating your first website to advanced customization options and integrations, this handbook aims to provide you with the knowledge and tools necessary to establish a strong online presence.

The journey of building and maintaining a successful website is an ongoing process that requires dedication, creativity, and a willingness to adapt to the ever-evolving digital landscape. However, with the right resources and a solid understanding of best practices, you can create a website that not only meets your current needs but also positions you for future growth and success.

As you continue to refine and expand your website, remember to prioritize the user experience, regularly update your content, and stay informed about emerging trends and technologies. Embrace the iterative nature of web development, and don't be afraid to experiment with new features or seek external support when needed.

The positive reviews we analyzed emphasized the importance of clear, step-by-step guidance, comprehensive coverage of topics, and the ability to understand and navigate the platform with ease. By incorporating these elements into your website development process, you can ensure a seamless and stress-free experience for yourself and your users.

Additionally, the negative reviews highlighted areas that could be improved, such as providing detailed instructions for specific tasks, ensuring mobile friendliness, and addressing gaps in content coverage. By learning from these critiques, you can avoid common pitfalls and create a more well-rounded and engaging website.

Remember, your website is a reflection of your brand, your vision, and your commitment to delivering value to your audience. Embrace the power of Wix and let your creativity shine through while adhering to best practices and industry standards.

As you commence on this exciting journey, keep in mind that the true measure of success lies not only in the initial launch of your website but also in its ability to adapt, evolve, and continue to meet the ever-changing needs of your target audience.

With dedication, perseverance, and a willingness to learn, you have the potential to create a truly remarkable online presence that sets you apart from the competition and leaves a lasting impression on your visitors.

www.ingramcontent.com/pod-product-compliance
Lightning Source LLC
Chambersburg PA
CBHW070318230526
45470CB00002B/933